AN

EASY

EXPLANATION

OF

BITCOIN

AND

BLOCKCHAIN

Thomas West

Table of Contents

INTRODUCTION

As the world continues transition into an online existence it comes as little surprise that systems such as Bitcoin and Blockchain have emerged. Bitcoin is what is known as a Cryptocurrency which is a digital currency that is not regulated by a central banking system. Cryptocurrencies provide secure and anonymous transactions which is a major contributor to its success. Without the need of a middleman to process transactions Bitcoin is also a cheap alternative to traditional currencies.

It can be said that the currency has revolutionized the way the online payment systems function in many ways. They are treated in the same way as your regular currency hence you need to be well aware about its usage before making any major transactions.

The price of this electronic currency is contstantly changing similar to that of the public stock market and is also reliant on the current market conditions.. It is best to not keep your savings in the form of Bitcoins as it would pose a great deal of risk. The best thing to do would be to convert the digital currency immediately to your local currency and never invest more in Bitcoin than you are able to lose.

It needs to be understood that payments that are made through the online currencies are irreversible and anonymous. The coins can only be refunded by the concerned individual or organization to which it has been sent so transactions should only be done with businesses you trust and have knowledge about. Otherwise, you will be at loss.

These days, many people make use of these electronic coins for trading. To obtain Bitcoin you can buy it from an online seller or if you have the knowledge and hardware you can mine them. Buying these can be quite a daunting task if you are not well aware about the processes associated with it but there are some websites that can help you a great deal when it comes to buying these coins. You can also seek the help of professional websites to trade based on the electronic currency easily. This is now turning out to be the best exchange trading method as it turns out to be a cost effective method as well.

CHAPTER 1
AN INTRODUCTION TO BITCOIN

Bitcoin has been in the news the last couple of weeks, but a lot of people are still unaware of them. Could Bitcoin be the future of online currency? This is just one of the questions, frequently asked about Bitcoin.

How Does Bitcoin Work?

Bitcoin is a type of electronic currency (CryptoCurrency) that is autonomous from tradi-tional banking and came into circulation in 2009.

According to some of the top online traders, Bitcoin is considered as the best known digital currency that relies on computer networks to solve complex mathematical problems, in order to verify and record the details of each transaction made.

The Bitcoin exchange rate does not depend on the central bank and there is no single authority that governs the supply of CryptoCurrency. However, the Bitcoin price depends on the level of confidence its users have, as the more major companies accept

Bitcoin as a method of payment, the more successful Bitcoin will become.

Benefits and Risks of Bitcoin

One of the benefits of Bitcoin is its low inflation risk. Traditional currencies suffer from inflation and they tend to lose their purchasing power each year, as governments continue to use quantative easing to stimulate the economy.

Bitcoin doesn't suffer from low inflation, because Bitcoin mining is limited to just 21 million units. That means the release of new Bitcoins is slowing down and the full amount will be mined out within the next couple of decades. Experts have predicted that the last Bitcoin will be mined by 2050.

Bitcoin has a low risk of collapse unlike traditional currencies that rely on governments. When currencies collapse, it leads to hyperinflation or the wipeout of one's savings in an instant.Bitcoin exchange rate is not regulated by any government and is a digital currency available worldwide.

Bitcoin is easy to carry. A billion dollars in the Bitcoin can be stored on a memory stick and placed in one's pocket. It is that easy to transport Bitcoins compared to paper money.

One disadvantage of Bitcoin is its untraceable

nature, as Governments and other organisations cannot trace the source of your funds and as such can attract some unscrupulous individuals.

Unlike other currencies, there are three ways to make money with Bitcoin, saving, trading and mining. Bitcoin can be traded on open markets, which means you can buy Bitcoin low and sell them high.

India has already been cited as the next likely popular market that Bitcoin could move into. Africa could also benefit hugely from using BTC as a currency-of-exchange to get around not having a functioning central bank system or any other country that relies heavily on mobile payments.

More people have accepted the use of Bitcoin and supporters hope that one day, the digital currency will be used by consumers for their online shopping and other electronic deals. Major companies have already accepted payments using the virtual currency. Some of the large firms include Fiverr, TigerDirect and Zynga, among others.

Bitcoin works, but critics have said that the digital currency is not ready to be used by the mainstream because of its volatility. They also point to the hacking of the Bitcoin exchange in the past that has resulted in the loss of several millions of dollars.

Supporters of digital currencies have said that there are newer exchanges that are supervised by financial experts and venture capitalists. Experts added that there is still hope for the virtual currency system and the predicted growth is huge.

CHAPTER 2
WHAT IS A CRYPTOCURRENCY?

A cryptocurrency is a decentralised payment system, which basically lets people send currency to each other over the web without the need for a trusted third party such as a bank or financial institution. The transactions are cheap, and in many cases, they're free. And also, the payments are pseudo anonymous as well.

As well as that, the main feature is that it's totally decentralised, which means that there's no single central point of authority or anything like that.

The implications of this is done by everyone having a full copy of all the transactions that have ever happened with Bitcoin. This creates an incredibly resilient network, which means that no one can change or reverse or police any of the transactions.

The high level of anonymity in there means that it's very hard to trace transactions. It's not totally impossible, but it's impractical in most cases.

In most cases when there's a crime online with

online payment systems,they tend to go to the authorities and, say, we can hand over this payment information or we can stop these transactions and reverse them. And none of that can happen with Bitcoin, so it makes it ripe for criminals, in theory.

In light of this, a lot of different agencies are researching into Bitcoin and looking at Bitcoin and trying to understand how it works and what they can do to police it. It's also been in the media quite a few times, and the media, being the media, like focus on the bad side of it.

So they focus very heavily on the crime with it. So if there's a theft or a scam or something like that, then they tend to blame it on Bitcoin and Bitcoin users.

So the most notable is probably Silk Road, which got taken down recently, and through their $1.2 billion worth of Bitcoins, went to pay for anything from drugs to guns to hit men to those sorts of things. And the media, again, very quickly to blame this on Bitcoins and say that it was the Bitcoin user's fault.

But there's actually very little evidence of the scale of the problem of crime with cryptocurrencies. We don't know if there's a lot or we don't know if there's a little. But despite this, people are very quick to brand it as a criminal thing, and they forget the legitimate uses, such as the fast and quick payment.

So the next question that I'd like to research as well is looking at the scale of the problem of crime with cryptocurrency. So by generating a log of known scams and thefts and things like that, we can then cross reference that with the public transaction log of all transactions and see just how much of the transactions are actually illegal and criminal.

By looking back at the crime logs, we can see which particular sorts of crime happen, and if it is actually the technology's fault, or is this just the same old crimes that we've been looking at before. And once we've consider these things, we can start to think about possible solutions to the issue of crime with Bitcoin.

And we can consider that the only suitable solution would be one that preserves the underlying values of the technology itself, which would be privacy and decentralisation.

A lot of focus from the media is to look at the criminal aspects of it. And they don't give enough value to the legitimate uses, because Bitcoin is a technology that enables fast, quick payments, which is useful to anyone that's ever paid for anything on the web.

If you are asked what the birth of cryptocurrency

would bring to the world of finance, the first thing that will probably cross your mind is what is cryptocurrency? This thought however, will only come to the mind of people who are not well versed with the existing online currencies.

But, if you are one of the few but dominant figures who know cryptocurrencies even if your eyes are closed, you would be able to answer the question more elaborately.

So to speak, the actual start of the turmoil existed when bitcoin was introduced to the world and eventually became the most famous and wanted cryptocurrency. This project was started primarily to answer the lingering complains of people whose money and assets are held by one centralized unit (and often intervened by the government itself) and whose transfers are limited and frozen at a timely basis.

With the start of Bitcoin, many had the option to acquire an online coin or currency that they can use similarly with fiat money.

Although acquiring it is tedious and requires resources, many were attracted to it from the very start because many were wanting to break away with the confinement of a single entity controlling everything else in terms of finance.

Slowly, Bitcoin started to gain actual monetary value and new types of cryptocurrencies came into existence as a possible answer to the problems that Bitcoin imposes and also to create their own currencies that people can opt to use as the one generated from the former is limited and hard to acquire.

Although cryptocurrency was not widely accepted, it slowly gained its momentum and now, many other businesses even accept it as a form of payment or exchange. The very same thing is slowly happening to new crypto currencies.

Although the profits are not guaranteed and the software running them is open-source, many still try to vie to acquire these currencies as another means of investment.

If this kind of merge between technology and finance continues to improve over time, it will be no wonder if more and more people will divert their attention to acquiring these coins and more businesses will open themselves to exchanging and accepting them as actual reward or trade for good and services.

Like everything else, the slow but steady approach of crypto currency could result to major changes in the way finance has been seen and treated in the past.

More people are opening their minds to the existence and stability of such platforms and many are craving to break away from the scrutinizing eyes of the governing bodies involved in the storage and exchange of their assets.

The future may seem dim this day but as more creative minds work together to make more convenience in the way finance and everything monetary is treated. Who knows maybe one day even fiat money can disappear for good.

CHAPTER 3
WHAT ARE OTHER UPCOMING CRYPTOCURRENCIES?

Everyone has heard of Bitcoin, even if they don't fully understand it. There are numerous other cryptocurrencies besides Bitcoin. There are 19 active cryptocurrencies, and most of these were released in the last couple of years.

Bitcoin has a considerable head start on the other offerings. Several cryptocurrencies are slight variations on the Bitcoin platform and may be more attractive to conventional financial institutions.

The first cryptocurrency to be welcomed by the banking industry will likely dominate the market. Which one will it be? Only the future will reveal the one that comes out on top.

Currently, these are the top five cryptocurrencies after Bitcoin:

1.Ripple. Ripple has a market capitalization of nearly $150 million. For comparison purposes, Bitcoin is almost $5 billion. This cryptocurrency was released in 2012 and has been making strong inroads into the banking industry and payment networks.

A "Bitcoin Bridge" permits Ripple currency holders to make payments to Bitcoin users without ever holding Bitcoins themselves. Some financial experts believe that Ripple will eventually overtake Bitcoin and become the dominant digital currency.

2. Litecoin. Litecoin is the third largest cryptocurrency with a market cap of $137 million. Charles Lee, a former Google employee, released Litecoin in 2011. This cryptocurrency is very similar to Bitcoin.

Litecoin offers several enhancements when compared to Bitcoin, including a higher limit on the maximum number of coins, improved user interface, and faster transaction approvals.

Several exchanges permit transactions of Litecoin with Bitcoin users and various conventional currencies, including US dollars, Euros, and Chinese Yuan.

3. Ethereum. The Ethereum market is half the size of Litecoin. Ethereum is challenging to understand, even for the experts. Ethereum combines the blockchain technology of Bitcoin with a programming language. This platform permits the construction of new applications to be developed.

4. Dash. Dash was started in 2014 as XCoin. You may have heard of XCoin or Darkcoin before they were rebranded to the name Dash. Dash is roughly one-tenth the size of Litcoin at $14 million. There are currently 6 million Dash coins in circulation.

Dash transactions are arguably more private than those of the previously mentioned currencies. Inputs from multiple users are needed to complete a transaction. Multiple identical outputs are also generated. These identical inputs and outputs shield the location and identity of the true parties.

5. Dogecoin. Dogecoin has approximately the same market capitalization as Dash. However, Dash currently has 6 million coins in circulation compared to the 102 billion coins of Dogecoin!

This crypto currency started as a joke, but quickly developed a loyal following. Coins are produced very quickly and have very little value, roughly $0.0001 per coin.

The Dogecoin community has been actively involved in fundraising for interesting causes, including the Jamaican Bobsled Team, a NASCAR driver, and building a well in Kenya. Several online exchanges exist to service those that wish to use Dogecoin.

The cryptography technology employed is similar to

that of Bitcoin and Litecoin and utilizes a private and public key system. There is no limit on the number of Dogecoins that can be produced. More than 5 billion coins are expected to be produced each year.

There's more going on in the cryptocurrency world than just Bitcoin. However, Bitcoin is the oldest and most well-known cryptocurrency in existence. The current Bitcoins in circulation are worth more than all of the other cryptocurrencies combined. It will be interesting to see what the future holds.

CHAPTER 4
WHAT IS BLOCKCHAIN AND WHY SHOULD YOU BE EXITED ABOUT IT?

If you've attempted to dive into this mysterious thing called blockchain, you'd be forgiven for recoiling in horror at the sheer opaqueness of the technical jargon that is often used to frame it.

So before we get into what a crytpocurrency is and how blockchain technology might change the world, let's discuss what blockchain actually is.

In the simplest terms, a blockchain is a digital ledger of transactions, not unlike the ledgers we have been using for hundreds of years to record sales and purchases.

The function of this digital ledger is, in fact, pretty much identical to a traditional ledger in that it records debits and credits between people. That is the core concept behind blockchain; the difference is who holds the ledger and who verifies the transactions.

With traditional transactions, a payment from one

person to another involves some kind of intermediary to facilitate the transaction. Let's say Rob wants to transfer £20 to Melanie. He can either give her cash in the form of a £20 note, or he can use some kind of banking app to transfer the money directly to her bank account.

In both cases, a bank is the intermediary verifying the transaction: Rob's funds are verified when he takes the money out of a cash machine, or they are verified by the app when he makes the digital transfer. The bank decides if the transaction should go ahead.

The bank also holds the record of all transactions made by Rob, and is solely responsible for updating it whenever Rob pays someone or receives money into his account. In other words, the bank holds and controls the ledger, and everything flows through the bank.

That's a lot of responsibility, so it's important that Rob feels he can trust his bank otherwise he would not risk his money with them. He needs to feel confident that the bank will not defraud him, will not lose his money, will not be robbed, and will not disappear overnight.

This need for trust has underpinned pretty much every major behaviour and facet of the monolithic finance industry, to the extent that even when it was discovered that banks were being irresponsible with our money during the financial crisis of 2008, the government (another intermediary) chose to bail them out rather than risk destroying the final fragments of trust by letting them collapse.

Blockchains operate differently in one key respect: they are entirely decentralised. There is no central clearing house like a bank, and there is no central ledger held by one entity. Instead, the ledger is distributed across a vast network of computers, called nodes, each of which holds a copy of the entire ledger on their respective hard drives.

These nodes are connected to one another via a piece of software called a peer-to-peer (P2P) client, which synchronises data across the network of nodes and makes sure that everybody has the same version of the ledger at any given point in time.

When a new transaction is entered into a blockchain, it is first encrypted using state-of-the-art cryptographic technology. Once encrypted, the transaction is converted to something called a block, which is basically the term used for an encrypted group of new transactions.

That block is then sent (or broadcast) into the network of computer nodes, where it is verified by the nodes and, once verified, passed on through the network so that the block can be added to the end of the ledger on everybody's computer, under the list of all previous blocks. This is called the chain, hence the tech is referred to as a blockchain.

Once approved and recorded into the ledger, the transaction can be completed. This is how cryptocurrencies like Bitcoin work.

Accountability and the removal of trust

What are the advantages of this system over a banking or central clearing system? Why would Rob use Bitcoin instead of normal currency?

The answer is trust. As mentioned before, with the banking system it is critical that Rob trusts his bank to protect his money and handle it properly. To ensure this happens, enormous regulatory systems exist to verify the actions of the banks and ensure they are fit for purpose.

Governments then regulate the regulators, creating a sort of tiered system of checks whose sole purpose is to help prevent mistakes and bad behaviour.

In other words, organisations like the Financial Services Authority exist precisely because banks can't be trusted on their own. And banks frequently make mistakes and misbehave, as we have seen too many times.

When you have a single source of authority, power tends to get abused or misused. The trust relationship between people and banks is awkward and precarious: we don't really trust them but we don't feel there is much alternative.

Blockchain systems, on the other hand, don't need you to trust them at all. All transactions (or blocks) in a blockchain are verified by the nodes in the network before being added to the ledger, which means there is no single point of failure and no single approval channel.

If a hacker wanted to successfully tamper with the ledger on a blockchain, they would have to simultaneously hack millions of computers, which is almost impossible.

A hacker would also be pretty much unable to bring a blockchain network down, as, again, they would need to be able to shut down every single computer in a network of computers distributed around the world.

The encryption process itself is also a key factor. Blockchains like the Bitcoin one use deliberately difficult processes for their verification procedure.

In the case of Bitcoin, blocks are verified by nodes

performing a deliberately processor- and time-intensive series of calculations, often in the form of puzzles or complex mathematical problems, which mean that verification is neither instant nor accessible.

Nodes that do commit the resource to verification of blocks are rewarded with a transaction fee and a bounty of newly-minted Bitcoins.

This has the function of both incentivising people to become nodes (because processing blocks like this requires pretty powerful computers and a lot of electricity), whilst also handling the process of generating - or minting - units of the currency.

This is referred to as mining, because it involves a considerable amount of effort (by a computer, in this case) to produce a new commodity. It also means that transactions are verified by the most independent way possible, more independent than a government-regulated organisation like the FSA.

This decentralised, democratic and highly secure nature of blockchains means that they can function without the need for regulation (they are self-regulating), government or other opaque intermediary. They work because people don't trust each other, rather than in spite of.

Let the significance of that sink in for a while and

the excitement around blockchain starts to make sense.

Smart contracts

Where things get really interesting is the applications of blockchain beyond cryptocurrencies like Bitcoin. Given that one of the underlying principles of the blockchain system is the secure, independent verification of a transaction, it's easy to imagine other ways in which this type of process can be valuable.

Unsurprisingly, many such applications are already in use or development. Some of the best ones are:

Smart contracts (Ethereum): probably the most exciting blockchain development after Bitcoin, smart contracts are blocks that contain code that must be executed in order for the contract to be fulfilled.

The code can be anything, as long as a computer can execute it, but in simple terms it means that you can use blockchain technology (with its independent verification, trustless architecture and security) to create a kind of escrow system for any kind of transaction.

As an example, if you're a web designer you could create a contract that verifies if a new client's website is launched or not, and then automatically release the funds to you once it is.

No more chasing or invoicing. Smart contracts are also being used to prove ownership of an asset such as property or art. The potential for reducing fraud with this approach is enormous.

Cloud storage (Storj): cloud computing has revolutionised the web and brought about the advent of Big Data which has, in turn, kick started the new AI revolution. But most cloud-based systems are run on servers stored in single-location server farms, owned by a single entity (Amazon, Rackspace, Google etc).

This presents all the same problems as the banking system, in that you data is controlled by a single, opaque organisation which represents a single point of failure. Distributing data on a blockchain removes the trust issue entirely and also promises to increase reliability as it is so much harder to take a blockchain network down.

Digital identification (ShoCard): two of the biggest issues of our time are identify theft and data protection. With vast centralised services such as Facebook holding so much data about us, and efforts by various developed-world governments to store digital information about their citizens in a central database, the potential for abuse of our personal data is terrifying.

Blockchain technology offers a potential solution to this by wrapping your key data up into an encrypted block that can be verified by the blockchain network whenever you need to prove your identity. The applications of this range from the obvious replacement of passports and I.D. cards to other areas such as replacing passwords. It could be huge.

Digital voting: highly topical in the wake of the investigation into Russia's influence on the recent U.S. election, digital voting has long been suspected of being both unreliable and highly vulnerable to tampering.

Blockchain technology offers a way of verifying that a voter's vote was successfully sent while retaining their anonymity. It promises not only to reduce fraud in elections but also to increase general voter turnout as people will be able to vote on their mobile phones.

Blockchain technology is still very much in its infancy and most of the applications are a long way from general use. Even Bitcoin, the most established blockchain platform, is subject to huge volatility indicative of its relative newcomer status.

However, the potential for blockchain to solve some

of the major problems we face today makes it an extraordinarily exciting and seductive technolo-gy to follow.

HOW BLOCKCHAIN TECHNOLOGY WORKS

New transactions (e.g. A would like to send ten bitcoins to B) are grouped within blocks. Each block is verified and validated by the "nodes" (network participants) or so-called "miners" using complex cryptotechnics which will depend on the type of blockchain.

In our bitcoin transaction example: the miners will verify that A is indeed owner of ten bitcoins and once this is confirmed, the transaction is validated and visible for B and the other network participants; B thus becomes the owner of said ten bitcoins.

Blockchain security methods use encryption technology. Network participants are incentivized to perform the verification and approval tasks, mostly by receiving fees or new cryptocurrencies. If a discrepancy is found, the block is rejected.

Otherwise validated transactions (in the block) are time-stamped and added to the chain, in a linear and chronological order, making a chain of transactions (or a chain of blocks) that shows every and all transactions in the history of that blockchain.

To be a part of a blockchain system, participating entities will each install and run some software that connects their computer or server to other participants in the network. By running this software, the participants act as individual validators, called network nodes.

A blockchain acts like a shared, replicated, append-only database node full copy of blockchain database network.When a node connects to the network for the first time, it will download a full copy of the blockchain database onto its computer or server.

The network of nodes manages the database, also known as the blockchain. The nodes are entry points for new data, as well as the validation and propagation of new data that have been submitted to the blockchain.

But in a distributed system with no golden source of truth, how does the network come to consensus, or agree on what data to write on the blockchain?

How do you resolve a situation where equivalent people can say conflicting things, but there is no boss to arbitrate?

The answer – using protocols. In a blockchain system there will be protocol, i.e. pre-agreed rules for technical and business validity of data to be written, and a rule to determine how consensus is achieved.

A block is created by grouping similar transactions together. These blocks are added in chronological order, in a way that resembles a chain, hence the name blockchain. The nodes then store these new blocks on the local blockchain database on their computer or server.

An intuitive solution is for nodes to act on time priority, keeping the first and rejecting the second. However different nodes may hear the messages in different orders.

The messages will propagate and some proportion of the network will believe A has happened (and B hasn't) and the rest of the network will believe B has happened (and A hasn't). The network is in an unstable state.

How is this resolved?

Each node is working on its own version of the truth. Whichever node gets to add the next block will propagate its version of events, and all nodes will read this and act on the new 'truth'.

Across a network, there is a possibility that two different blocks are added at the same time by different nodes, creating a fork in the chain. In this case, there is a 'consensus rule' that helps nodes figure out which is the block they should believe.

In bitcoin, the rule is called the 'longest chain rule' – each node acknowledges the legitimacy of both contender blocks and the situation resolves when the next block is built on one of the contenders. The longer chain becomes part of the de-facto blockchain.

One node may receive two pieces of mutually conflicting data. For example A is, "I sell all my shares to Alice," and B is, "I sell all my shares to Bob." Each node will have to keep one and reject one as they cannot both logically coexist.

CHALLENGES AND ISSUES IN THE USE OF BLOCKCHAIN

As the blockchain ecosystem evolves and different use cases emerge, organizations in all industry sectors will face a complex and potentially controversial array of issues, as well as new dependencies.

Awareness and understanding

The principal challenge associated with blockchain is a lack of awareness of the technology, especially in sectors other than banking, and a widespread lack of understanding of how it works. This is hampering investment and the exploration of ideas.

Organization

The blockchain creates most value for organizations when they work together on areas of shared pain or shared opportunity – especially problems particular to each industry sector. The problem with many current approaches, though, is that they remain stove-piped: organisations are developing their own blockchains and applications to run on top of them.

In any one industry sector, many different chains are therefore being developed by many different organisations to many different standards. This defeats the purpose of distributed ledgers, fails to harness network effects and can be less efficient than current approaches.

Culture

A blockchain represents a total shift away from the traditional ways of doing things – even for industries that have already seen significant transformation from digital technologies. It places trust and authority in a decentralized network rather than in a powerful central institution. And for most, this loss of control can be deeply unsettling.

It has been estimated that a blockchain is about 80 per cent business process change and 20 per cent technology implementation. This means that a more imaginative approach is needed to understand opportunities and also how things will change

Cost and efficiency

The speed and effectiveness with which blockchain networks can execute peer-to-peer transactions comes at a high aggregate cost, which is greater for some types of blockchain than others.

This inefficiency arises because each node performs the same tasks as every other node on its own copy of the data in an attempt to be the first to find a solution.

For the Bitcoin network, for example, which uses a proof-of-work approach in lieu of trusting participants in the network, the total running costs associated with validating and sharing transactions on the public ledger are estimated to be as much as $600 million a year and rising.

This total does not include the capital costs associated with acquiring specialist mining hardware.

Blockchains are something of a productivity paradox, therefore. At the scale of the entire network the process is significantly productivity enhancing, but requires a certain 'critical mass' of nodes. Yet, even so, individual nodes can work extremely hard and may not contribute very much to the network overall.

Therefore, decisions about implementing blockchain applications need to be carefully thought through.

The returns to individual processing nodes – either individuals in a public blockchain or organisations in a sector-wide blockchain – may diminish as the network grows in size. This means that blockchain applications must harness network effects to deliver value to consumers or to sectors at large.

Regulation and governance

Regulations have always struggled to keep up with advances in technology. Indeed, some technologies like the Bitcoin blockchain bypass regulation completely to tackle inefficiencies in conventional intermediated payment networks. One of the other challenges of the blockchain approach, which was also one of its original motivations, is that it reduces oversight.

Centralized systems, particularly in financial services, also "act as shock absorbers in times of crisis" despite their challenges and bottlenecks. Decentralized networks can be much less resilient to shocks, which can impact participants directly, unless careful thought is given to their design.

There is thus a strong argument for blockchain applications to work within existing regulatory structures not outside of them, but this means that regulators in all industries have to understand the technology and its impact on the businesses and consumers in their sector.

Security and privacy

While cryptocurrencies like Bitcoin offer pseudonymity (Bitcoin transactions are tied to 'wallets' rather than to individuals), many potential applications of the blockchain require smart transactions and contracts to be indisputably linked to known identities, and thus raise important questions about privacy and the security of the data stored and accessible on the shared ledger.

Some argue that while no technology is completely secure, no one has yet managed to break the encryption and decentralised architecture of a blockchain.Identities created within a blockchain would be unique and offer a higher level of assurance that the party was who they claim to be.

But these claims do not take away from the need for every organisation adopting the technology to consider how privacy and security can inform the design. In particular, driving public acceptance of blockchain applications will likely mean proactively framing the discussion of privacy around concepts of value, security and trust.

BLOCKCHAIN AS AN ALTERNATE OF CURRENCY

Blockchain represents the currency itself, e.g Bitcoin, Litecoin, Peercoin etc. In order to use these currencies (which are just hashes in the system), the protocol has to be followed and blockchain architecture is used as an underlying database where every transaction between two parties is stored.

So, every change of ownership is marked in the blockchain and it can be traced back until its creation (Coin creation, i.e introduction of new coins is also determined by the protocol).

This implies: To check whether a person possesses a specific coin, one has to check the blockchain and see if a specific person got a specific coin from somebody or not.

Also the blockchain technology makes it impossible to double-spend the coin, because every change is written in the block. Much like regular currency Bitcoins are decomposable into smaller units. The smallest unit in Bitcoin is 1 Satoshi which is 10−8 Bitcoins (or abbreviated BTC).

The most appealing characteristic of Bitcoin as a currency is the level of anonymity it provides its users. Unlike traditional financial institutions, where information related to the transaction is limited only to the parties involved, Bitcoin transactions are made public.

That is, we can see the amount of Bitcoins transferred from one party to another, but the identities of the parties involved are completely hidden from the public eye. Derived from public keys, Bitcoin addresses are pseudonymous in that they could represent anyone on the Internet and are not linked to anyone's identity.

A new public/private key pair is generated for each Bitcoin address, and any user can sign up for multiple addresses without divulging any personal information.

Overall, Bitcoin has several defining characteristics.

Although transactions are not completely anonymous, they do offer a high level of pseudonymity. All transactions are publicly announced via the blockchain, which ensures that no double spending can occur, and are irreversible once they have been validated.

Additionally, Bitcoin has low transaction costs and a finite money supply. Most importantly, Bitcoin is neither controlled nor mediated by a 3rd party institution, making it a fully deregulated and decentralized cryptocurrency.

CHAPTER 5
SIMPLE WAYS TO BUY AND INVEST IN BITCOIN

Bitcoin is a decentralized, peer to peer, digital currency system, designed to give online users the ability to process transactions via digital unit of exchange known as Bitcoins. In other words, it is a virtual currency.

The Bitcoin system was created in the year 2009 by an undisclosed programmer(s). Since then, Bitcoin has garnered huge attention as well as controversy as an alternative to US dollar, Euros and commodity currencies such as gold and silver.

Rise to Popularity

Bitcoin had not attained much attention in the world of business and finance before the year 2009. It rose to prominence in the 2011-2012 period when it gained over 300%. Bitcoin has had a 400% growth in its value since the August of last year. As a result, venture capital firms and investors around the world continue to pay importance to the cryptocurrency.

In the first half of 2014, venture capital firms invested $57 million in Bitcoin in the first quarter, followed by another $73 million in the second quarter amounting to a total of $130 million, which is 50% greater than last year's total of $88 million. This is a complete contrast to the scenario in 2012 where Bitcoin firms amassed a relatively meagre sum of $2.2 million.

These statistics prove beyond doubt that Bitcoin is worth your investment, which begs the question, how can you buy and invest in Bitcoin?

A guideline for novice investors in Bitcoin

The easiest and least complicated method to invest in Bitcoin is by purchasing bitcoins. There are a lot of established firms, mainly in the US as well as abroad, who are involved in the business of buying and selling bitcoins, abbreviated as BTC.

Coinbase

If you are living in the U.S. then Coinbase is the place you're looking for. Coinbase provides it's clients with BTC at an estimated mark up of 1% over the existing market price. Residents of the United States have the option to sync their Coinbase wallets with their bank accounts.

As a result, future payment transfers are made hassle free. This company also gives you the option of automatic bitcoin buying from time to time. For instance, if you're interested to purchase $50 in bitcoins at the beginning of each month, Coinbase allows you to set up an auto buy for that amount.

Be mindful of the terms and conditions before you begin to use this service. If you have subscribed to an automatic bit coin service, then you will not be able to control the price at which the BTC is bought every month.

Note that Coinbase is does not function as a Bitcoin exchange i.e. you buy and sell the coins directly from the firm. Since the firm has to source the coins from other buyers, you may face delays or disruptions when laying orders during fast market moves.

BitStamp

BitStamp suits the requirements of a conventional bitcoin exchange. Bitcoin acts as an intermediary which allows you to trade with other users and not the company itself.

Here the liquidity is higher and you always have a good chance to find someone who is willing to trade with you. There is an initial fee of 0.5% which can be reduced to 0.2% if you trade $150,000 in a period of 30 days.

Alternative ways to purchase Bitcoins

Local Bitcoins

Exchanging isn't the only method of investment in bitcoins. Local Bitcoins is often used to buy BTC offline. The website is designed to link potential buyers and sellers. The bitcoins are locker from the seller in an escrow and can only be released to buyers.

Buying bitcoins offline isn't always very reliable or safe. Hence it's preferable to meet the sellers during daytime and let a friend tag along with you just in case things go south.

Bitcoin is not just a modern trend. Venture capital firms consider Bitcoin to be a decent substitute to conventional currency in the long run. There are cointless ways for you to enter the sphere of bitcoin investment.

As mentioned before, Coinbase, BitStamp and Local Bitcoins are the most popular channels for investing in bitcoin in the United States. Do your homework and find out which avenue ticks all your boxes.

How to invest in Bitcoin

Wondering if you should invest in Bitcoin? If you've been around any kid of financial news lately, you've no doubt heard about the meteoric rise in the world's most well-known cryptocurrency.

Well here's a few things you should know about Bitcoin before you invest.

Pros of Bitcoin

1 Easy To Send Money

Because it's decentralized, this also means that you can send a friend Bitcoin (money) on the other side of the world in seconds without having to go through a bank intermediary (and pay the banking fees).

This fact alone makes Bitcoin very popular. Instead of waiting for a wire transfer which can take days, you can send your payment in seconds or minutes.

2 Limited Supply

There are only 21 million Bitcoins that will ever be mined. This limits the amount of Bitcoin that can ever be produced. This is like saying a government cannot print money because there is a limited supply of bills - and they won't print anymore.

When there is a set supply your purchasing power is preserved and the currency is immune to runaway inflation.

This limited supply has also helped to contribute to the rise in the price of Bitcoin. People don't want a currency that can be printed - or inflated - into infinity at the whim of a greedy government.

3 Private

Most people think that Bitcoin is completely anonymous. But actually it's not anonymous - it's more private. All Bitcoin transactions ever made can be seen on the Blockchain - the public Bitcoin ledger.

But your name and identifying details behind the transaction are not seen. Each transaction is linked to an address - a string of text and characters. So while people might see your address - there is no way to link that address to you.

A lot of people who don't like their banks spying on them (or telling them how much of their own money that they can or can't move), really like this privacy feature.

4 Cheaper to Transact

Many businesses have to take Visa or MasterCard

these days to stay competitive. However these cards take some rather substantial fees out of each sales transaction.

But a merchant who accepts Bitcoin doesn't pay these hefty fees - so it puts more money in their pockets.

So those are some of the main pros of Bitcoins. What about the cons?

Cons of Bitcoin

1 Risky - Price Fluctuations

Bitcoin is famous for rising slowly over months - and then falling 20 - 50% over a couple of days.

Because it's being traded 24 hours a day 7 days a week, the price is always fluctuating. And all it takes it some bad news - like the news of the Mt Gox hack a few years ago - to send the price tumbling down.

So basically it's not stable - and there are a lot of unknowns out there that can affect the price. The rule here is this: don't put any money into Bitcoin that you can't afford to lose.

2 Slowing Transaction Speeds

Bitcoin is starting to run into problems with slower transaction speeds and higher transaction fees.

Other cryptocurrencies have come along that are faster and cheaper.

The Bitcoin miners are working on the problem. However until these issues are resolved, you can expect the price to be extremely volatile.

3 Bitcoin Transactions Not Reversible

Unlike a credit card charge, Bitcoin transactions are not reversible. So if you send Bitcoin to the wrong address - you can't get it back.

Also, there are a lot of tales from people who have lost their Bitcoin wallet address (through hacking, phones being stolen, virus-infected computers, etc.) and they've completely lost their coins. There's no way to get them back.

For this reason, you really need to know what you're doing and take the time to research how to buy and store your coins properly if you want to invest in Bitcoins - or any other cryptocurrency.

So those are some of the things to consider before investing in Bitcoin. Basically while Bitcoin has a lot of great things going for it - and while it has the potential to change financial transactions as we know it - there is still a lot of risk. There are a lot of unknowns out there still.

If you do decide to buy, take your time and research your options. Don't buy from just any seller. Some of them are trustworthy and run a great business. But there are others that will overcharge you and may not even deliver your coins.

Be safe and do your research first. Find a trusted seller with a stellar reputation - there are quite a few of them out there. And remember the golden rule here - never invest more than you can afford to lose.

CHAPTER 6
HOW TO TRADE BITCOIN

There are plenty of reasons why you should consider trading the currency. Some of these reasons include:

Ease of entry: Unlike the stock market and other trading channels, there are almost no barriers to entry into the Bitcoin market. All you need to do is identify a seller that you can buy from. If interested in selling, identify a buyer, and you are ready to go.

Global: You can trade the currency from any part of the world. This means that a person in China can buy or sell Bitcoin to a person in Africa or any other place. This makes the currency significant as it isn't affected by the economy of a single country.

It's volatile: Just like the other currencies in the foreign exchange market, Bitcoin is highly volatile. This means that it quickly changes its price due to slight shifts in the economy. If you take advantage of the changes, you can make huge profits.

24/7 trading: Unlike the stock market that operates

during the business hours, Bitcoin trading happens the entire day and night. The trading limitations are only on you-not on time.

If interested in getting into the market, there are plenty of ways you can use to get the currency. Some of the ways you can use include:

Buying on an exchange: Here you need to get into the marketplace, and you will find people looking to sell the currency. You should identify a reputable seller and place an order.

Transfers: You can also get Bitcoin from a friend. Here a friend needs to send you the currency via an app located on the computer or phone.

Mining: This is the traditional way of getting the coins. In this method, you use the computer to solve complex math puzzles. After successfully completing a puzzle you are rewarded with the coins. While this method is free, it's usually time-consuming.

Bitcoin is a currency just like any other. It can not only be used to buy and sell, but can be used for investing and sharing, and can even be stolen.

While the initial introduction of the technology came with a desktop program, it can now be directly operated through a smartphone application, which allows you to immediately buy, sell, trade or even cash your bitcoins for dollars.

Investment with bitcoins has become very popular, with major sums of money being put in every day. As a new investor, the rules remain the same as investing with real cash. Do not invest more than you can afford to lose, and do not invest without a goal. For every trade, keep certain milestones in mind.

The 'buy low and sell high' strategy is not as easy implemented as said. A great way to succeed faster when you decide to trade bitcoins, however, is to learn the technicalities. Like cash investments, there are now several bitcoin charting tools to record the marketing trends and make predictions to help you make investment decisions.

Even as a beginner, learning how to use charting tools and how to read charts can go a long way. A normal chart will usually include the opening price, the closing price, the highest price, the lowest price and the trading range, which are the essentials you need before making any sale or purchase.

Other components will give you different information about the market. For example, the 'order book' contains lists of prices and quantities that bitcoin traders are willing to buy and sell.

Moreover, new investors will often quickly open unprofitable positions. With this, however, remember that you have to pay an interest rate for every 24 hours that the position is kept open, with the exception of the first 24 hours that are free.

Therefore, unless you have sufficient balance to cover the high interest rate, do not keep any unprofitable position open for more than 24 hours.

While bitcoin trading still has its drawbacks, like transactions taking too long to complete and no reversing option, it can benefit you greatly with investing, provided that you take small steps in the right direction.

The Bitcoin Market

The Bitcoin market is the market where Bitcoins are traded. When you have Bitcoins, you can use them for purchasing almost anything for which this currency is accepted.

There are certain kinds of trades for which Bitcoins are the only form of payment that is widely accepted. If you want to acquire that specific good, then Bitcoins will be required to complete the transaction.

When you step into the Bitcoin market, the first thing you need to learn is how to acquire Bitcoins.

The first option is to purchase them. It will take little effort to do it this way. The second option is to mine them.

Mining takes place on software that performs certain mathematical equations for which the trader is rewarded some Bitcoins. This is quite time taking and many traders say that it bears a small portion of fruit.

Process of Purchasing Bitcoins

• In order to become a part of the Bitcoin market, you will need wallet software. You can also get an online service instead. There are online wallet services available in all major countries so you will not face any trouble in setting up your wallet account.

• You will have to link your wallet to your bank account to let the purchasing begin. This can take a few days depending upon your wallet service.

• Once your bank account is linked, you will see a buy Bitcoins link in the software window. This is going to be simple. Once the transaction is completed, the Bitcoins will be transferred to your wallet.

The Bitcoin market works on the same strategies that are used in any other type of trading market.

When the price of Bitcoins becomes low, it's a signal to buy them. When the price becomes high, you can sell them to earn profit.

Mining can be hard, but all traders should still try it from time to time. It is a bit slow and so you will have to be patient. You will need Bitcoin mining software. There are even mining pools. You have to simply decrypt a block with the joint effort of a mining group. You will then get Bitcoins according to your contribution.

Keep in mind, the value of Bitcoins goes up and down within seconds. If you don't make the right move at the right time, you can lose a significant portion of your investment. A good thing is that once you fully understand the basics, you can reap lots of profits from this form of trading.

CHAPTER 7
WHERE TO BUY BITCOIN

If you're looking to get into the game of Bitcoin and hold your own coins, there are many options available. Here are some of the different methods available for acquiring some Bitcoin of your own.

Buy them from an exchange

One of the most common ways to acquire bitcoins is through an exchange. Websites like Bitstamp, BTC-E, or Cavirtex here in Canada, allow you to purchase Bitcoin. They don't sell Bitcoin themselves, but how it works is the exchanges pair you as a buyer with a seller who's selling for whatever price you're looking for.

This sounds like a great option, and in some ways it is, but it has its disadvantages as well.

One of the major ones is that the exchanges require you to add your personal information to them via Know Your Client legislation that's present in many countries in regards to currency-related businesses.

This might not be a concern for everyone, but in a

post-NSA scandal era, it's becoming more and more clear, at least to me, that data you put out there is more accessible than you think.

I might be a little paranoid, but who knows what might happen in the future. After all, just ten years ago the idea that the government is spying on everything we do was purely the realm of tin foil hat conspiracy theorists, and now it's just common knowledge. Who knows what's next?

As you can tell, I'm not a big fan of the exchanges. The idea that I have to give up my personal information to an entity which might have to release that information seems to go against the spirit of Bitcoin.

Fortunately, there are other options.

Mine them

Of course, there's only one place Bitcoins really come from; mining. Every Bitcoin you'll ever own, see, or hear about, was at one point mined via the Bitcoin mining network.

If you find yourself in possession of a mining rig, go ahead and mine away! Or if you have a computer fast enough to make it worthwhile, that's cool too.

But be careful! If your computer isn't cooled

properly, you run the risk of overheating it, which could potentially brick it.

Frankly, mining with your computer isn't really worth it. Not anymore. As the mining difficulty increases, it becomes more and more difficult to gain any profit from it. And unless you have a dedicated mining rig, your chance of getting any sort of return from mining is pretty low.

Some argue that mining is on its way out, and even buying a dedicated mining rig isn't really a valid option anymore. I disagree, but that's a topic for another day.

Buy them from a private broker

If you're able to find a private broker, you can hook up with them and exchange. This has some obvious benefits, but it also has drawbacks.

First off, it's completely anonymous. Even if you meet in person, there's no reason you need to use your real name, or any details about yourself other than your wallet number so they can transfer the funds to you. And if you pay cash, the banks can't trace it either. So if that's a concern for you, you're in business.

But of course with anonymity comes some risk as well. Dealing through an exchange, the risk of getting ripped off is lower. Of course, exchanges have disappeared in the past, taking everyone's Bitcoins with them, but the bigger, more established exchanges have had time to build their brand and prove themselves as more trustworthy.

You may pay a price premium for that anonymity as well. From my experience, it can be as much as 15-20% higher than average exchange prices. But again, if anonymity is important to you, that's a small price to pay.

When you trade with someone anonymously, you don't have the security of the exchanges. They could be legit and honest, but they could just as easily be shady and willing to rip you off.

That said, buying from a private broker is my preferred method of purchasing Bitcoin. But it's important to have safety measures in place, otherwise you're leaving yourself open to getting burned.

Accept them as payment for goods and services

This one is so obvious, yet often people forget about it. Amidst all the investors getting involved with Bitcoin and the excitement around the movement, it's easy to forget that Bitcoin is not just a hot commodity or high value stock. It's designed as a form of currency. And if you run a business, you can accept Bitcoin as payment instead of cash.

There are many different businesses which accept Bitcoin as a form of payment. If you live in Canada, check out this directory of businesses which accept Bitcoin.

In fact, several directories have popped up to help people find local businesses which accept Bitcoin. And, if you're a denizen of the web (and if you're reading this, you obviously are), there are tons of places which accept Bitcoin as payment. Tiger Direct, Reddit, and WordPress are just a few of them.

In short, there are many different ways to acquire Bitcoin. Some are easier than others, but with so many options, you're certain to find something which works for you. Get into the game now, don't miss out!

How to Buy a Bitcoin

Here are some simple steps to buy bitcoin:

• Find A Wallet

First of all, you have to find an e-wallet. It is basically a store or a provider that offers software from where bitcoins can be bought, stored, and traded. You can easily run it on your desktop, laptop, and even smartphones.

• Sign Up

Next, you have to sign up with e-wallet. You will make an account that will let you store your bitcoins. The e-wallet trader will offer you a chance to convert your local currency into bitcoin. Therefore, the more local currency you have, the more bitcoins you can purchase.

• Connect Your Bank Account

After signing up, the trader has to connect his bank account with his trading account. For this purpose, some verification steps are to be performed. Once the verifications are performed, then you can start purchasing bitcoins and get started.

• Buying And Selling

Once you are done with your first purchase, your bank account will be debited and you will get the bitcoins. Selling is done in the same way purchasing is done. Keep in mind that the price of bitcoin changes time after time. The e-wallet you are working with will show you the current exchange rate. You should be aware of the rate before you buy.

Mining bitcoin

There is another way through which you can purchase bitcoins. This process is known as mining. Mining of bitcoins is similar to discovering gold from a mine. However, as mining gold is time consuming and a lot of effort is required, the same is the case with mining bitcoins.

You have to solve a series of mathematical calculations that are designed by computer algorithms to win bitcoins for free. This is nearly impossible for a newbie. Traders have to open a series of padlocks in order to solve the mathematical calculations.

In this procedure, you do not have to involve any kind of money to win bitcoins, as it is simply brainwork that lets you win bitcoins for free. The miners have to run software in order to win bitcoins with mining.

Bitcoin is a digital currency that is here to stay for a long time. Ever since it has been introduced, the trading of bitcoin has increased and it is on the rise even today. The value of bitcoin has also increased with its popularity. It is a new type of currency, which many traders are finding attractive just because of its earning potentials.

At some places, bitcoins are even being used for purchasing commodities. Many online retailers are accepting bitcoin for the real time purchases too. There is a lot of scope for bitcoin in the coming era so buying bitcoins will not be a bad option.

CHAPTER 8
WHAT ARE THE BENEFITS OF BITCOIN OVER REGULAR CURRENCIES

Bitcoin is a form of currency existing only in the digital world. The technology was created by an individual hiding under an identity named Satoshi Nakamoto. To this day, the creator/creators of the system never materialized, maintaining an anonymous status.

Bitcoins are not printed like traditional currencies as there are no physical representations for the cryptocurrency; it is produced by users and numerous businesses through a process called mining. This is where dedicated software solves mathematical problems in exchange for the virtual currency.

A user takes control of it using electronic devices, which also serves as medium to complete transactions with the help of numerous platforms. It is also kept and secured with the employment of virtual wallets.

Characteristics of Bitcoin

Bitcoin has the characteristics of traditional currencies such as purchasing power, and investment applications using online trading instruments. It works just like conventional money, only in the sense that it can only exist in the digital world.

One of its unique attributes that cannot be matched by fiat currency is that it is decentralized. The currency does not run under a governing body or an institution, which means it cannot be controlled by these entities, giving users full ownership of their bitcoins.

Moreover, transactions occur with the use of Bitcoin addresses, which are not linked to any names, addresses, or any personal information asked for by traditional payment systems.

Every single Bitcoin transaction is stored in a ledger anyone can access, this is called the blockchain. If a user has a publicly used address, its information is shared for everyone to see, without its user's information of course.

Accounts are easy to create, unlike conventional banks that requests for countless information, which may put its users in jeopardy due to the frauds and schemes surrounding the system.

Furthermore, Bitcoin transactions fees will always be small in number. Apart from near-instant completion of processing, no fees are known to be significant enough to put a dent on one's account.

Uses of Bitcoin

Apart from its abilities to purchase goods and services, one of its known applications features its use for a number of investment vehicles. This includes Forex, trading Bitcoins, and binary options platforms. Furthermore, brands offer services that revolve around Bitcoin as currency.

Clearly, Bitcoin is as flexible as traditional legal tenders. Its introduction provides every individual with new beneficial opportunities with its ease of use and profit making capabilities.

It's not an actual coin, it's "cryptocurrency," a digital form of payment that is produced ("mined") by lots of people worldwide. It allows peer-to-peer transactions instantly, worldwide, for free or at very low cost.

Bitcoin was invented after decades of research into cryptography by software developer, Satoshi Nakamoto (believed to be a pseudonym), who designed the algorithm and introduced it in 2009. His true identity remains a mystery.

This currency is not backed by a tangible commodity (such as gold or silver); bitcoins are traded online which makes them a commodity in themselves.

Bitcoin is an open-source product, accessible by anyone who is a user. All you need is an email address, Internet access, and money to get started.

Bitcoin is mined on a distributed computer network of users running specialized software; the network solves certain mathematical proofs, and searches for a particular data sequence ("block") that produces a particular pattern when the BTC algorithm is applied to it. A match produces a bitcoin. It's complex and time- and energy-consuming.

Only 21 million bitcoins are ever to be mined (about 11 million are currently in circulation). The math problems the network computers solve get progressively more difficult to keep the mining operations and supply in check.

This network also validates all the transactions through cryptography.

Internet users transfer digital assets (bits) to each other on a network. There is no online bank; rather, Bitcoin has been described as an Internet-wide distributed ledger. Users buy Bitcoin with cash or by selling a product or service for Bitcoin.

Bitcoin wallets store and use this digital currency. Users may sell out of this virtual ledger by trading their Bitcoin to someone else who wants in. Anyone can do this, anywhere in the world.

There are smartphone apps for conducting mobile Bitcoin transactions and Bitcoin exchanges are populating the Internet.

How is Bitcoin valued?

Bitcoin is not held or controlled by a financial institution; it is completely decentralized. Unlike real-world money it cannot be devalued by governments or banks.

Instead, Bitcoin's value lies simply in its acceptance between users as a form of payment and because its supply is finite.

Its global currency values fluctuate according to supply and demand and market speculation; as more people create wallets and hold and spend bitcoins, and more businesses accept it, Bitcoin's value will rise.

Banks are now trying to value Bitcoin and some investment websites predict the price of a bitcoin will be several thousand dollars in 2014.

What are its benefits?

There are benefits to consumers and merchants that want to use this payment option.

1. Fast transactions - Bitcoin is transferred instantly over the Internet.

2. No fees/low fees -- Unlike credit cards, Bitcoin can be used for free or very low fees. Without the centralized institution as middle man, there are no authorizations (and fees) required. This improves profit margins sales.

3. Eliminates fraud risk -Only the Bitcoin owner can send payment to the intended recipient, who is the only one who can receive it. The network knows the transfer has occurred and transactions are validated; they cannot be challenged or taken back.

This is big for online merchants who are often subject to credit card processors' assessments of whether or not a transaction is fraudulent, or businesses that pay the high price of credit card chargebacks.

4. Data is secure -- As we have seen with recent hacks on national retailers' payment processing systems, the Internet is not always a secure place for private data. With Bitcoin, users do not give up private information.

a. They have two keys - a public key that serves as the bitcoin address and a private key with personal data.

b. Transactions are "signed" digitally by combining the public and private keys; a mathematical function is applied and a certificate is generated proving the user initiated the transaction. Digital signatures are unique to each transaction and cannot be re-used.

c. The merchant/recipient never sees your secret information (name, number, physical address) so it's somewhat anonymous but it is traceable (to the bitcoin address on the public key).

5. Convenient payment system -- Merchants can use Bitcoin entirely as a payment system; they do not have to hold any Bitcoin currency since Bitcoin can be converted to dollars. Consumers or merchants can trade in and out of Bitcoin and other currencies at any time.

6. International payments - Bitcoin is used around the world; e-commerce merchants and service providers can easily accept international payments, which open up new potential marketplaces for them.

7. Easy to track -- The network tracks and permanently logs every transaction in the Bitcoin

block chain (the database). In the case of possible wrongdoing, it is easier for law enforcement officials to trace these transactions.

8. Micropayments are possible - Bitcoins can be divided down to one one-hundred-millionth, so running small payments of a dollar or less becomes a free or near-free transaction. This could be a real boon for convenience stores, coffee shops, and subscription-based websites (videos, publications).

Still a little confused? Here are a few examples of transactions:

Bitcoin in the retail environment

At checkout, the payer uses a smartphone app to scan a QR code with all the transaction information needed to transfer the bitcoin to the retailer. Tapping the "Confirm" button completes the transaction. If the user doesn't own any Bitcoin, the network converts dollars in his account into the digital currency.

The retailer can onvert that Bitcoin into dollars if it wants to, there were no or very low processing fees (instead of 2 to 3 percent), no hackers can steal personal consumer information, and there is no risk of fraud. Very slick.

Bitcoins in hospitality

Hotels can accept Bitcoin for room and dining payments on the premises for guests who wish to pay by Bitcoin using their mobile wallets, or PC-to-website to pay for a reservation online. A third-party BTC merchant processor can assist in handling the transactions which it clears over the Bitcoin network.

These processing clients are installed on tablets at the establishments' front desk or in the restaurants for users with BTC smartphone apps. (These payment processors are also available for desktops, in retail POS systems, and integrated into foodservice POS systems.) No credit cards or money need to change hands.

These cashless transactions are fast and the processor can convert bitcoins into currency and make a daily direct deposit into the establishment's bank account.

It sounds good - so what's the catch?

Business owners should consider issues of participation, security and cost.

• A relatively small number of ordinary consumers and merchants currently use or understand Bitcoin. However, adoption is increasing globally and tools and technologies are being developed to make participation easier.

• It's the Internet, so hackers are threats to the exchanges. The Economist reported that a Bitcoin exchange was hacked in September 2013 and $250,000 in bitcoins was stolen from users' online vaults. Bitcoins can be stolen like other currency, so vigilant network, server and database security is paramount.

• Users must carefully safeguard their bitcoin wallets which contain their private keys. Secure backups or printouts are crucial.

• Bitcoin is not regulated or insured by the US government so there is no insurance for your account if the exchange goes out of business or is robbed by hackers.

• Bitcoins are relatively expensive. Current rates and selling prices are available on the online exchanges.

The virtual currency is not yet universal but it is gaining market awareness and acceptance. A business may decide to try Bitcoin to save on credit card and bank fees, as a customer convenience, or to see if it helps or hinders sales and profitability.

CONCLUSION

Bitcoin is widely known as a decentralized payment system, which allows for the transfer of funds across borders at virtually no costs and without external control.

As such, it can serve as a new backbone technology for depository institutions, increasing the speed and efficiency of inter-bank transfers and making it easier for banks to convert funds from one currency to another.

On the technical level, Bitcoin is a so-called trustless payment system, enabling people or institutions that do not know each other (and therefore do not trust each other) to exchange value directly, without the need for any trusted authority or centralized clearing house.

It is trustless not because there is no trust in the transactions, but because things simply cannot go wrong in the first place.

Bitcoin has its own rules and regulation programmed directly into its fabric: trust is delegated to the network itself, where all transactions are public and verifiable by everyone. The sustainers of the network —the so-called miners or validators— act as an insurance for the actual execution of these transactions.

This is important for two main reasons:

1. It allows for a more distributed network of exchange, where people can exchange value directly with one another, instantaneously, and without relying on any potentially corrupted, unreliable, or monopolistic (rent-taking) financial intermediary.

2. It provides a mechanism for banking the unbanked —enabling those who are currently cut off from the financial system, often because they have no trust to offer, to enter the global economy.

This is particularly relevant for the most vulnerable persons who have not been able to access financial services, such as immigrants and migrants, as well as the swaths of populations that live under corrupt, authoritarian or unstable governments and political systems.

The same technology can also be used to vastly improve the remittance market, while enabling a greater degree of financial inclusion. Currently, the remittance fees charged by multinational corporations, which maintain a monopoly on international value transfer networks, amount to a large portion of the global financial aid sent to developing countries.

The World Bank estimates that even a reduction of a few percentage points in the costs of remittance would save billions of dollars to the overall remittance costs.

Of course, given the lack of a central regulatory authority, Bitcoin also comes along with a number of challenges.

Given the ease of access to this decentralized peer-to-peer payment system, Bitcoin provides new opportunities for criminal activities, including tax-evasion and money-laundering (as shown by the case of SilkRoad, where Bitcoin was used as a near-anonymous payment system for the sale of illegal drugs).

The response, in the US at least, has been to regulate decentralized virtual currencies, by regulating the commercial operators (such Bitcoin exchanges and wallet providers) as if they were regular financial operators or money transmitters —and thus require them to comply with Anti Money Laundering (AML), Know Your Customers (KYC) and money transmission laws.

Note that these same regulations, when applied into the blockchain space, may undermine standard expectations of financial privacy.

There is therefore, a growing need to reconsider the impact of existing AML/KYC regulations (drafted in an era of closed "black boxes") in light of this new technological framework that provides tools for for better governance and fraud prevention —thereby reducing or even eliminating the need for such an extensive set of (onerous) regulations.

Most importantly, it is important to remember that the real innovation of Bitcoin is not the currency itself, rather than its underlying technology —the blockchain, a decentralized trust platform. Bitcoin is only one out of many possible applications of this new technology, which can be incorporated into many different types of applications that operate similarly to the Bitcoin blockchain in some respects, and differently in others.

Accordingly, before regulating Bitcoin as a virtual currency, it is necessary to understand the real opportunities that its underlying technologies provides, without getting sidetracked by the cryptocurrency hype.

In particular, the blockchain gives rise to new possibilities that were previously impossible – or impractical – and are therefore not fully accounted for in the current regulatory regime.

Looking at financial applications, blockchain technologies can be used to execute more secure and trustless transactions: for example, creating free and secure escrow system with built-in multisignature features.

Blockchain technologies can also provide a more efficient and secure securities market, by enabling both automatic settlement and clearance by peers, without a centralized clearinghouse. The U.S. Securities and Exchange Commission has understood this and now allows for securities to be issued directly onto the blockchain.

The derivatives market can also be made more efficient and transparent, by encoding the terms of a derivative instrument directly into the blockchain, automating both transactions and payment.

A direct monetary connection can be established linking the actual value of collaterals with the derivative, which makes liquidity-freezes like those of 2008 impossible.

Beyond financial applications, the blockchain can also be used as a decentralized and tamperproof registry of titles, such as a land registry (as the current experiment in Honduras might show) or as a way to record any contractual or licensing agreements, such as intellectual property.

In the context of Internet of Things and smart cities initiatives, it is estimated that there will be over 50 billion interconnected devices in 2020, each needing to communicate and transact with one another. Because no central public or private authority could possibly act as the central clearing for all of these transactions, the blockchain provides an efficient and secure solution to govern and execute trillions of transactions in a trustless manner.

Finally, the most recent versions of the blockchain make it possible to execute complex code, in a decentralized and deterministic manner, without relying on any central server.

This allows for the creation of decentralized applications (such as decentralized market places, or decentralized prediction markets), which are neither owned nor controlled by anyone, but simply subsist on the blockchain, and are executed each time someone interacts with them.

The benefit is that no one can alter the operations of that code —which is actually incorruptible. Besides, as blockchains enable new forms of value creation and distribution within a particular network, they opens up new possibilities for new establishing of decentralized organisation and the generation of social and economic coordination, with greater transparency, lower cost and more equality of access.

However, the problem is that there is no one to be held responsible for the operations of that blockchain code, for better or worse. These applications do not reside in any actual jurisdiction and could therefore be constructed to be agnostic to any jurisdiction's rules.

As with the Internet, it will be nearly impossible to stop all unlawful activities that will be made possible by blockchain technologies. Yet, while governments might not be able to halt the use of these technologies, they could at least limit the adoption, and regulate the development of these technologies.

Blockchain technology already plays a crucial role in the financial services sector

Originally created as the technology to support digital currency 'bitcoin', blockchain has been seized upon by the financial services sector, where it is playing a crucial role in tracking and authenticating transactions.

Of course, if financial services businesses can find advantages from the adoption of blockchain technology, then you may well be wondering what it can offer other sectors. Some examples are already beginning to emerge.

Insurance is one area of financial services where blockchain is an obvious fit. The sector is employing blockchain technology when registering luxury assets to help prevent theft and fraud.

One project, which involves Interpol, insurers and diamond distributors, is working to stem the flow of 'blood diamonds' into the precious-stones market. Blockchain provides what is hoped will be a tamper-proof record of the provenance of diamonds.

In the health sector, blockchain is being considered as a solution to the counterfeiting of drugs. The creation of a decentralised database of medical records, which would give patients more control over their personal data, is also being explored.

How to assess the value of blockchain to your business

While the hype around blockchain may suggest it can be applied to any business, it isn't always a suitable solution. So how do you ensure it is a viable option for your business and that it can truly add competitive advantage? And how do you implement it?

These considerations can be broken down into

three key stages:

1. Training

The training stage is about obtaining hands-on experience of how blockchain works, where it can be applied and how to leverage it, often through case histories.

2. Diagnosis of the business case

Diagnosis of the cost and benefits of using blockchain, in the context of a business case, is also vital – not least because adopting new technologies will likely involve the replacing of a legacy system or generating a new business model.

3. Development

The development stage will require you to understand which is the right solution for you. Right now, there are no one-off 'plug-and-play' products on the market, so every solution must be tailor-made.

Of course, this process is not straightforward and you will likely face many challenges along the way. Implementing a change programme of this magnitude is time-consuming.

With blockchain, once a protocol is developed, you must be prepared to go back and forth to fine tune the product. And because blockchain as a concept is still evolving, new advances are emerging all the time.

There are other industry-related challenges to consider too, such as sector-specific laws and government regulations. For industry-wide projects, it's always best to bring in the regulators from the beginning.

Although interest from early adopters such as China, Estonia, India, Singapore and the UK is particularly strong, many governments and regulators aren't ready for blockchain and in those cases we have to find a solution without them.

All of this means collaboration with experts and a willingness to 'test and adapt' is a must.

Blockchain will create huge disruption in many sectors and, potentially, see some firms leave the market. But by bringing in the right expertise and adopting a collaborative approach, it might also be the technology that will help you to steal a march on your competitors.